CELEB ★ ★

FASHION MODEL

CLARE HIBBERT

W
FRANKLIN WATTS
LONDON • SYDNEY

First published in 2010 by
Franklin Watts
338 Euston Road
London NW1 3BH

Franklin Watts Australia
Level 17/207 Kent Street
Sydney NSW 2000

ISBN: 978 0 7496 9261 2

Dewey classification number: 746.9'2'092

J746.
92

A CIP catalogue record for this book is available from the British Library.

Planning and production by Discovery Books Limited
Managing editor: Laura Durman
Editor: Clare Hibbert
Designer: D.R. Ink
Picture research: Colleen Ruck
Thanks to Lauren Ferguson and Danielle Huson

Photo acknowledgements: Getty Images: cover (Thomas Concordia/WireImage), pp 1 and 21 (Randy Brooke/WireImage), 4 (Studio Fernanda Calfat), 5 (Gareth Cattermole), 6–7 (Jemal Countess/WireImage), 7 (Venturelli/WireImage), 9 (MJ Kim), 10 (Slaven Vlasic), 12 (Barry King/WireImage), 13 (Peter Kramer), 14 (Dave Benett), 15 (Chris Jackson), 18 (Nick Harvey/ WireImage), 20 (Pascal Le Segretain), 22 (Dave Hogan), 23 (Samir Hussein), 24–25 (SGP Italia srl/WireImage), 25 (JP Yim/WireImage), 26 (Mario Rossi/WireImage), 28 (Jon Levy/ AFP), 29 (Gianfranco Calcagno/FilmMagic); Rex Features: pp 8, 19 (Sipa Press); Shutterstock Images: pp 3 (Loke Yek Mang), 16–17 and 31 (Goncharuk).

Printed in China

Franklin Watts is a division of Hachette Children's Books, an Hachette UK company.
www.hachette.co.uk

To the best of its knowledge, the Publisher believes the facts in this book to be true at the time of going to press. However, due to the nature of celebrity, it is impossible to guarantee that all the facts will still be current at the time of reading.

CONTENTS

Fact

Bündchen has a fortune of around $150 million — and in 2008 she earned around $35 million.

Bündchen at Sao Paolo Fashion Week, Brazil.

GISELE BÜNDCHEN

CELEB BIO

Date of birth **20 July 1980**

Origins **Horizontina, Brazil**

Height **1.79m**

Hair colour **Brown**

Eye colour **Blue**

UK agency **IMG London**

Key catwalk shows **Ralph Lauren, Versace, Valentino, Chloé, Victoria's Secret**

Achievements **Appearing on the cover of *Vogue* four times in one year (1999)**

'I'm a workaholic. I've been doing my job a long time.'

The lives of fashion models seem incredible. They show off the latest designer clothes, and their faces are on the covers of glossy magazines. It's hard work, though, and incredibly competitive.

FASHION

TODAY'S BIGGEST MODEL

SUPERMODELS

CITY MOVER

CELEB BIO

Date of birth **30 November 1989**

Origins **Atlanta, Georgia, USA**

Height **1.75m**

Hair colour **Dark brown**

Eye colour **Brown**

UK agency **Viva London**

Key catwalk shows **Dolce & Gabbana, Issey Miyake, Hermès, Marc Jacobs, Stella McCartney**

Achievements **Appearing on the cover of US Vogue in May 2007, as one of the next crop of supermodels**

CHANEL IMAN

Backing every fashion model is an agency. Modelling agencies work behind the scenes, putting models in touch with the advertising people and fashion designers who give them jobs to do.

GETTING A CONTRACT

Would-be models work hard to get a modelling contract with one of the top agencies. A small number of fortunate wannabes are discovered by scouts. Others have to get noticed. They may send in photographs or attend open auditions or agency modelling shows.

WINNING WORK

Chanel Iman signed to US agency Ford Models at the age of 12. But her career really took off five years later, when she won third place in the agency's 2006 Supermodel of the World competition. That got her noticed! Soon after, she made her debut at New York Fashion Week.

AGENCY WORK

Ford Models has put forward Iman's name for catwalk work with such big-name designers as Louis Vuitton, John Galliano, Yves Saint Laurent (YSL) and Christian Lacroix. Iman has also appeared in advertising campaigns for high-street stores Gap and Benetton.

TEEN TRAINING

Like Iman, most models start their careers in their teens and agencies train them on the job. Iman was home-schooled because she wanted qualifications as well as a modelling career. She hopes to do some fashion designing herself, some day, and has already become involved in the music business.

Chanel Iman walking the catwalk for Blumarine at Milan Fashion Week.

Fact

Chanel's mum named her after the French fashion designer, Coco Chanel.

'I'm still a regular girl. I go to basketball and [American] football games.'

LISA SNOWDON

In recent years, would-be models have found a new platform for getting noticed – televised talent contests. Reality shows such as *Next Top Model* give young models a chance to launch their career with a bang.

TALENT ON TV

First aired in 2003, *America's Next Top Model* was the brainchild of ex-model Tyra Banks. It launched the careers of Adrianne Curry, Eva Marcille and Joanie Dodds, among others. Since then, spin-off shows have been broadcast in more than 30 different countries. *Britain's Next Top Model* began in 2005 and was hosted by British model Lisa Butcher. Lisa Snowdon took over as presenter and head judge in 2006.

MODEL CAREER

Lisa Snowdon was signed by Premier Model Management at the age of 19 and appeared in various ad campaigns during the 1990s, including ones for Lynx men's deodorant and Neutrogena face-care products.

AWAY FROM MODELLING

In 1997 Snowdon released an album, *Spell it Out*, but it flopped. Her next venture, fronting VH1's *All Access*, proved that she had talent as a TV presenter. With her inside knowledge of the fashion business, she was the perfect choice for *Britain's Next Top Model*.

DISCOVERIES

With her fellow judges, Snowdon has helped to discover a new generation of models. Lianna Fowler, Lauren McAvoy and Alex Evans are all destined for great things. In a sister show, *Britain's Missing Top Model*, eight women with disabilities competed for a modelling contract. Its winner, Kelly Knox, is now working as a model.

Fact

In 2008 Snowdon and Brendan Cole finished third in *Strictly Come Dancing*. Lisa was the first celebrity to score top marks in the Latin and ballroom dances.

'There are way prettier girls than me, and there always will be.'

CELEB BIO

Date of birth **23 January 1972**

Origins **Welwyn Garden City, Hertfordshire, UK**

Height **1.78m**

Hair colour **Brown**

Eye colour **Blue**

UK agency **Money Management**

Key magazine shoots *Marie Claire, Cosmopolitan, Eve, Vogue*

Achievements **Becoming known as the British Tyra Banks**

Snowdon at the launch party for the first series she hosted of *Britain's Next Top Model.*

Rocha on the catwalk showing off part of Isaac Mizrahi's Spring 2009 collection.

A model's looks are his or her fortune. It is part of the job to take care of these looks. Just as it does for everyone else, that means following a sensible diet and taking regular exercise.

COCO ROCHA

FAST FOOD

Models sometimes find it difficult to eat well. During fashion shoots or catwalk shows there may only be soggy sandwiches on offer! Fizzy drinks and chocolate are tempting for a quick energy lift. Long-term, however, healthy eating is the only way to maintain a sensible weight and glowing, clear skin.

SIZE ZERO

The fashion business is often criticised for promoting too-skinny models, especially those who are US size 0 (UK size 4). Some are naturally slim, but others have eating disorders. Unable to see their bodies as they really are, they damage their health as they try to become thinner.

UNDER PRESSURE

The Canadian model Coco Rocha is among those catwalk stars who have spoken out against the pressures to look thin. She recounted how people in the business urged her to lose weight, saying: 'We don't want you to *be* anorexic, we just want you to look it.'

SHAPING THE FUTURE

Rocha has suggested that designers should make samples (the outfits for their shows) in larger sizes. Rocha herself is a UK size 8 (US size 4). She keeps in shape by playing sports and Irish dancing – and famously once opened a Jean Paul Gaultier show by jigging down the catwalk!

CELEB BIO

Date of birth **10 September 1988**

Origins **Toronto, Ontario, Canada**

Height **1.78m**

Hair colour **Brown**

Eye colour **Blue**

UK agency **Storm Model Management**

Key catwalk shows **Anna Sui, Marc Jacobs, Christian Lacroix, Emanuel Ungaro**

Achievements **Appearing on the cover of Italian *Vogue* aged just 17.**

Fact

Rocha teams up with Heidi Klum to fight the forces of evil in a popular online comedy series called *Spiked Heel*.

'Once a week I go out with some of my buds and play a game of soccer.'

Fact

Schenkenberg speaks five languages: Swedish, English, Dutch, Italian and French.

'Do I consider myself beautiful? No!'

One of the shots of Schenkenberg rollerskating that launched his career.

MARCUS SCHENKENBERG

Most of the models who become celebrities are women, but male modelling is also big business. Like their female counterparts, male models need dedication and discipline to make it to the top.

MAKING IT

The Swedish-Dutch model Marcus Schenkenberg was one of the trailblazers for male modelling. The story of his discovery in 1989 by the photographer Barry King – he was rollerskating in Venice Beach, California – has entered fashion folklore.

MUSCLE MAN

Schenkenberg is famed for his muscular body. He runs, plays basketball and trains with weights in the gym. His highest-profile advertising campaign, for Calvin Klein underwear, showed off his 'washboard' abs (abdominal muscles).

MODELLING

Schenkenberg was the first male model to appear on the front cover of a fashion mag – *Harper's Bazaar.* Valentino, Donna Karan, Versace, Armani and Iceberg have all used him as a model, both on the catwalk and in advertising campaigns. He's also appeared in adverts for Absolut vodka and Joop perfume.

CELEB BIO

Date of birth **4 August 1968**

Origins **Stockholm, Sweden**

Height **1.93m**

Hair colour **Brown**

Eye colour **Brown**

UK agency **Storm Model Management**

Key catwalk shows **Versace, Armani, Hugo Boss, Vivienne Westwood**

Achievements **First male supermodel**

Schenkenberg on the catwalk for the 'Dressed to Kilt' fashion show.

BEYOND MODELLING

In 1997 Schenkenberg published a book, *Marcus Schenkenberg, New Rules*. It included stories about him modelling, contributions from colleagues, friends and family – and lots of glossy photos. Schenkenberg still models, but is also a TV presenter, film actor and workout instructor.

PHOTOGRAPHERS

Photographers play a crucial part in the fashion business. The most successful create images that are valued works of art — and that can define the look of a particular model or generation of models.

BEHIND THE CAMERA

Fashion photographers usually work for themselves. Magazine editors commission them to organise 'shoots' where sets of pictures are taken for magazine features. They also work on advertising campaigns. Shoots may take place in the studio or outside, in exotic and not-so-exotic locations!

WORKING WITH HERB

Over her career, the Sudanese-born model Alek Wek has been shot by some of the biggest names in the business. Herb Ritts, who died of AIDS in 2002, was the leading fashion photographer of the 1980s and 1990s. One of his most enduring images is of Wek after she had been body-painted by the artist Joanne Gair.

A TOUGH START

Alek Wek's name means 'black spotted cow' in her native Dinka language. Wek fled Sudan aged 14, because of civil war. She was studying at the London College of Fashion when a Models One scout saw her in a London market. Her breakthrough job was appearing in the music video for the Bond theme, 'GoldenEye'.

IN FRONT OF THE CAMERA

Wek moved to the United States in 1996. In addition to Ritts, American photographers Bruce Weber, Annie Leibovitz, Steven Meisel and Steven Klein all took pictures of her. She also worked with the world-famous Peruvian photographer, Mario Testino.

Alek Wek with Mario Testino, after he won Most Stylish Photographer at the British Style Awards.

Fact

Mario Testino is the world's highest-paid photographer. As well as models, his subjects have included ex-Prime Minister Margaret Thatcher, Diana, Princess of Wales, Madonna, Gwyneth Paltrow and Robbie Williams.

ALEK WEK

Alek Wek poses for a portrait in the Ritz Carlton Hotel, Washington DC.

'Just don't try and tell me that only one look is beautiful.'

CELEB BIO

Date of birth **16 April 1977**

Origins **Wau, Sudan**

Height **1.80m**

Hair colour **Black**

Eye colour **Brown**

UK agency **Storm Model Management**

Key catwalk shows **Gucci, Fendi, Jean Paul Gaultier, Vivienne Westwood, Chanel**

Achievements **Working for the US Committee for Refugees' Advisory Council**

NAOMI CAMPBELL

Magazine editors wield enormous power in the modelling world. Appearing on the front cover of one of the world's top fashion magazines is a sure sign that a model has made it.

READERS

The biggest fashion publications are *Glamour*, *Vogue* and *Elle*. *Glamour* is the UK's favourite women's magazine, with a circulation of around half a million. *Vogue* is bought by around 240,000 readers in the UK and 1.2 million in the United States.

COVER STORIES

The use of a celebrity or a supermodel on the cover of a fashion magazine can really boost sales. The British supermodel Naomi Campbell has posed for more than 500 magazine covers during her long career.

TAKING OFF

The daughter of a dancer, Campbell studied ballet at the Italia Conti Academy, a drama school in London. After she was discovered, aged 15, her modelling career took off immediately. In April 1986 she appeared on the cover of *Elle*.

BIG SIX

Vogue played a big part in turning models into celebrities during the 1990s. Its use of Campbell helped her to become one of the 'Big Six' (see page 5). She also hit the magazine pages in glossy ads and has represented a huge range of companies, from Burberry to H&M.

CELEB BIO

Date of birth **22 May 1970**

Origins **London, UK**

Height **1.75m**

Hair colour **Black**

Eye colour **Brown**

UK agency **Independent Models**

Key catwalk shows **Hermès, Givenchy, Marchesa, Dolce & Gabbana, Anna Sui, Matthew Williamson**

Achievements **Being called one of the top three (or trinity of) supermodels, along with Christy Turlington and Linda Evangelista**

'I work very hard and I'm worth every cent.'

AGYNESS DEYN

Models sometimes describe themselves as clothes horses. Their job is to show off clothes to their best advantage. Without models, where would the fashion designers be?

CUSTOM CLOTHES

The world of haute couture is a strange one. Twice a year, designers produce a range of clothes for the upcoming season. High-fashion clothes can't be bought off a rail in a shop. The designer makes them to order, so they exactly fit the measurements of the customer. Haute couture outfits can cost tens or even hundreds of thousands of pounds.

READY-TO-WEAR

Sometimes none of a designer's made-to-measure clothes actually sell. The catwalk show is really just to get publicity for the brand. Coverage of the catwalk shows helps people to recognise the designer's name, and makes them want to buy the designer's perfumes or ready-to-wear collections.

DEYN AND THE DESIGNERS

Designers often have favourite models, trusting them to make the outfits look spectacular. The British model Agyness Deyn has walked the catwalk for many fashion houses, including Anna Sui, Oscar de la Renta, Versace and Missoni. The designer with whom she is most linked, though, is Henry Holland of House of Holland. The pair grew up together! She's a regular now on the Channel 4 fashion programme Henry co-hosts, called *Frock Me*.

'This season [Henry Holland's] new collection is going to be major.'

Henry Holland and Agyness Deyn.

DEYN'S BACKGROUND

Deyn spent most of her teens working in a fish and chip shop – a far cry from the glamorous world of fashion! In 1999 she won a modelling contest in the local newspaper and decided to move to London. Two years later a scout spotted her out shopping. She had her first magazine cover – for Italian *Vogue* – in November 2006.

Deyn at a tribute party for the punk designer Stephen Sprouse, who died in 2004.

CELEB BIO

Real name **Laura Hollins**

Date of birth **16 February 1983**

Origins **Manchester, UK**

Height **1.73m**

Hair colour **Blonde**

Eye colour **Blue**

UK agency **Models One**

Key catwalk shows **Jean Paul Gaultier, Michael Kors, Anna Sui, House of Holland**

Achievements **Replacing Angelina Jolie as the face of Shiseido perfume**

In 2008 Agyness Deyn was guest editor for an issue of *i-D* magazine. For one of the features she interviewed famous fashion designer Dame Vivienne Westwood.

19

LAKSHMI MENON

Fashion shows are theatrical events. There's dramatic lighting and evocative music but the centrepiece is the catwalk – the stage upon which the models show off the clothes.

Menon walks the catwalk for Jean Paul Gaultier in Paris.

ON SHOW

Known as the runway in the United States, the catwalk is long and thin to allow an up-close view for as many members of the audience as possible. Front-row seats are reserved for magazine editors, celebrities and other influential folk.

TRIPS AND SLIPS

Sashaying along the catwalk can be a nerve-wracking experience. Even in impossibly-high heels, models are expected not to falter, wobble or trip – although most make at least one catwalk blunder during their career. Some catwalks are incredibly slippery!

CATWALK SCHEDULE

Indian model Lakshmi Menon documented her experience of New York Fashion Week in a video diary in February 2009. In the space of one day, Menon walked in three different shows: for designers Ohne Titel, Diane von Furstenberg and Alexander Wang.

ADS AND SHOWS

Menon made her name internationally in 2006 after landing the Swatch ad campaign. She modelled exclusively for Givenchy during the Autumn 2008 season and took part in ad campaigns for Givenchy and Max Mara. She's also modelled for Carolina Herrera, Badgley Mischka, Stella McCartney, Jean Paul Gaultier and Dolce & Gabbana.

CELEB BIO

Date of birth **1 January 1981**

Origins **Bangalore, India**

Height **1.78m**

Hair colour **Black**

Eye colour **Brown**

UK agency **Storm Model Management**

Key catwalk shows **Ralph Lauren, Vera Wang, Issey Miyake**

Achievements **First Indian model to appear solo on the cover of Vogue (India)**

'You need a lot of patience, waiting for things to happen.'

Menon models for Zac Posen during New York Fashion Week.

HYE PARK

Fact

Park studied biology at the University of Utah and wanted to be a biologist for ...

Date of birth **17 January 1985**

Origins **Seoul, South Korea**

Height **1.78m**

Hair colour **Dark brown**

Eye colour **Brown**

UK agency **Take 2 Model Management**

Key catwalk shows **Prada, Chanel, Dolce & Gabbana, Miu Miu, Louis Vuitton**

Achievements **Being the second Asian model ever to walk for Prada**

Sometimes designers know just what look they want to create. Other times, they put their trust in the stylists. Armies of hairdressers and make-up artists work behind the scenes to make the catwalk collections as eye-catching as possible.

A model's hair style must complement the clothes, not distract from them. Long hair is more versatile because it can be worn up or down. Pinning it up is a must if the stylist needs to draw attention to the neckline of an outfit – to show off a high collar, for example.

Korean model Hye Park has sported many different hair styles during her modelling career, from slicked back to bouffant. It is very important for models to have a strong face, or 'look', so that they can carry off the different styles. For catwalk shows, models sometimes have to use temporary dyes or spray-in colour. They may even wear wigs!

Make-up styles go in and out of fashion just as clothes do. Edgier clothes can take dark, dramatic make-up. Park can carry a natural look, but she's fantastic in heavy make-up, too.

Park's international modelling career began in 2005 at the age of 20. She appeared in Italian *Vogue* and walked for Prada and Miu Miu during Milan Fashion Week. She has since appeared in many magazine editorials and has been featured in ad campaigns for H&M, Gap and Dolce & Gabbana.

Park models for Rebecca Taylor in New York.

Fact

Beckford gave Britney Spears a ride through Paris on his motorbike in her video 'Toxic', 2003.

Beckford photographed for a campaign for Pirelli.

'Fashion is very important to me and I am a product of fashion.'

TYSON BECKFORD

High-profile advertising campaigns are the most sought-after jobs in fashion. Stars may be paid millions of pounds to become the exclusive face of a product. Competition is fierce, and some contracts go to movie actors rather than professional models.

POLO FRONT MAN

During the 1990s, Tyson Beckford was the main model for Ralph Lauren's Polo Sport clothing and fragrance ranges. Beckford, who comes from mixed Jamaican and Chinese-American parentage, met Ralph Lauren through the fashion photographer Bruce Weber. Before that, he'd been modelling in a hip-hop magazine called *The Source*.

FAME AND FORTUNE

Beckford was paid more than half a million dollars a year by Ralph Lauren for his Polo Sport adverts. He also represented Gucci, Tommy Hilfiger, Calvin Klein and Guess Raw Denim. Perfume campaigns bring fame as well as money. Since they appear in a wide range of publications, not just fashion magazines, they really boost a model's profile.

TV HOST

Beckford's face is familiar around the world and he has carved out a successful career after modelling. He hosts the US reality TV programme, *Make Me a Supermodel*, and acts as mentor to the male contestants. The show offers a prize of $100,000 and a modelling contract. Contestants get the chance to follow in Beckford's footsteps, modelling and promoting products. Winners include Holly Kiser and Branden Rickman.

FACE FOR FILM

Beckford has also taken on roles in various films, proving himself as an actor and producer. On occasion he has even played himself onscreen, notably in *Zoolander*, a spoof movie about the competitive – and vain! – world of male models.

'I like creating images.'

KATE MOSS

Very few modelling careers last for decades. Some models find alternative careers in the worlds of pop music, TV or film. Others launch their own clothes or beauty products.

Moss modelling in New York in 1995.

MAGAZINE FAVOURITE

Kate Moss is one of the all-time great models. Her first magazine cover was for *The Face*, when she was just 15. Moss had been spotted by a scout in an airport, coming home from a holiday in the Caribbean. In her 20-year career, she has featured on more than 25 British *Vogue* covers.

FASHION DESIGNER

In addition to her modelling, Moss has become a successful businesswoman. In 2006 she was asked to design for the high-street fashion chain, Topshop. Her first collection, launched in May 2007, sold out in hours. Moss does not actually design the clothes all by herself, but her experienced eye, ability to set trends and,

of course, her celebrity, make her contribution invaluable. She has lent her name to a series of fragrances, too.

MAKING MUSIC

Moss has made waves in the music business, appearing in videos for such diverse acts as Elton John and Marianne Faithful. She's sung on tracks for indie bands Primal Scream and Babyshambles, and while dating Babyshambles' Pete Doherty, Moss co-wrote some songs for the band.

PARTY ON

Despite scandals in her personal life, Moss is still in demand on the catwalk. She lost some advertising contracts after revelations of cocaine use, but she remains the face of a range of brands, including Rimmel and Virgin Mobile.

CELEB BIO

Date of birth **16 January 1974**

Origins **Croydon, Greater London, UK**

Height **1.69m**

Hair colour **Brown**

Eye colour **Hazel**

UK agency **IMG London**

Key catwalk shows **YSL, Chanel, Chloé, Christian Dior**

Achievements **Being named Best-Dressed Woman by** *Glamour* **magazine, 2008; making Breakthrough Breast Cancer a household name with her T-shirt campaign**

Moss poses in the window of Topshop's flagship store at the launch of her first clothing range.

Fact

In 2008 the artist Marc Quinn made a golden statue of Moss, entitled *Siren*. Containing 50kg of gold, the piece was valued at £1.5 million.

GLOSSARY

advertising The business of letting consumers know about products.

anorexic Describes someone with anorexia, an eating disorder that makes sufferers lose dangerous amounts of weight.

brand The name of a product or range of products. Many fashion brands take the name of the designer.

catwalk Known as the runway in the USA, the long, thin platform (or area of floor) upon which a model shows off clothes at a fashion show.

circulation In the world of magazines, describes how many copies are sold.

commission To ask someone to do something for money.

debut First appearance.

diet The food that a person eats. The term sometimes describes an eating plan that restricts intake of food.

eating disorder An illness that makes the sufferer damage their health by eating too little or too much.

editor On a magazine, the person who is responsible for what's inside.

fashion week A week of fashion shows in a particular city. The most important fashion weeks, held twice yearly, are in New York, London, Milan and Paris.

feature In a magazine, an article or pages that show models wearing clothes that share the same designer or promote the same 'look'.

haute couture The business of creating very expensive, high-quality fashionable clothes, often made exactly to the customer's measurements.

home-schooled Describes someone taught privately at home, rather than at school.

made-to-measure Describes clothes that are custom-made to fit the wearer.

modelling agency A company that finds work for models.

open audition An audition (for example, for a place with a modelling agency) that is open to anyone – prospective models just have to turn up.

photoshoot A session when a photographer takes pictures for a particular project.

ready-to-wear Describes fashionable clothes that are bought already made, rather than specifically made-to-measure.

reality TV An unscripted TV show starring people (being themselves, not acting) facing challenges, such as living together in a house, taking part in a talent contest or trying out a new job.

samples Clothing made by a designer to show off a new collection, worn by fashion models on the catwalk and in magazines.

scout Someone employed by a modelling agency to find new talent.

season In the world of fashion, there are two seasons: Autumn/Winter and Spring/Summer. Designers show off their coming Autumn/Winter collection between January and March, and the next year's Spring/Summer collection between September and November.

shoot Short for photoshoot.

size 0 The US women's clothing size that is equal to a UK size 4. Sizes vary between manufacturers but on average this size means being roughly 80cm around the chest, 60cm around the waist and 85cm around the hips.

supermodel A highly paid and highly successful fashion model.

talent contest A competition that rewards the most gifted contestant. Winners of modelling contests need good looks, poise and a professional approach.

trade show An exhibition at which everyone in a particular business shows off what they have been doing and what they are planning to do.

visionary Someone with good ideas for the future.

FURTHER INFORMATION

BOOKS

21st Century Lives: Fashion Designers by Liz Gogerly (Wayland, 2004)

21st Century Lives: Supermodels by Liz Gogerly (Wayland, 2008)

Read All About It: Fashion by Adam Hibbert (Franklin Watts, 2004)

Trailblazers: Fashion by David Orme and Helen Orme (Ransom Publishing, 2008)

Tyra Banks: From Supermodel to Role Model by Anne E. Hill (Lerner Publications, 2009)

Virtual Apprentice: Fashion Designer by Don Rauf and Monique Vescia (Facts on File, 2009)

WEBSITES

http://www.fashion.net/howto/fashionmodel
A guide to becoming a fashion model, including information about finding an agency.

http://www.londonfashionweek.co.uk
The official website for London Fashion Week.

http://nymag.com/fashion
New York magazine's guide to fashion and style, with information on models, designers and fashion shows.

http://www.rubbishmag.com
The website of *The Daily Rubbish*, London Fashion Week's newspaper.

INDEX